W9-BFE-367

The True Story of the
DECLARATION OF INDEPENDENCE

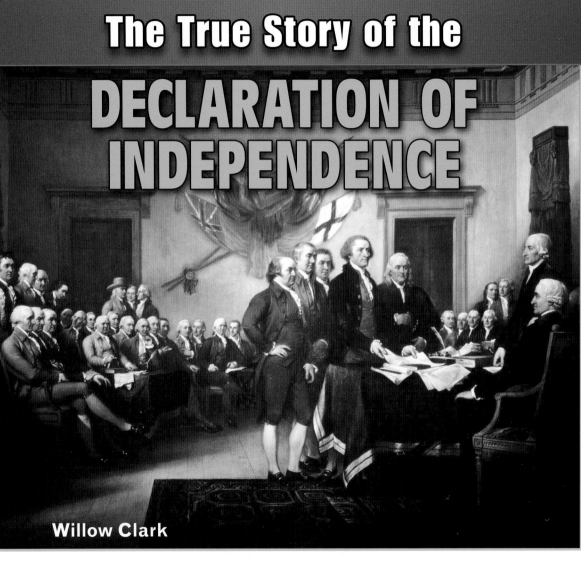

Willow Clark

PowerKiDS press.

New York

Published in 2013 by The Rosen Publishing Group, Inc.
29 East 21st Street, New York, NY 10010

First Edition

Editor: Amelie von Zumbusch
Book Design: Colleen Bialecki

Photo Credits: Cover Van D Bucher/Photo Researchers/Getty Images; p. 5 KidStock/Blend Images/Getty Images; p. 7 English School/The Bridgeman Art Library/Getty Images; p. 9 William Barnes Wollen/The Bridgeman Art Library/Getty Images; p. 11 Tony Spuria/Shutterstock.com; p. 13 Sanham, Paul (20th Century)/Private Collection/The Bridgeman Art Library; p. 15 Superstock/Getty Images; p. 17 © iStockphoto.com/Roel Smart; p. 19 American School, (18th Century)/Private Collection/Peter Newark American Pictures/The Bridgeman Art Library; p. 20 Louis Charles Auguste Couder/The Bridgeman Art Library/Getty Images.

Library of Congress Cataloging-in-Publication Data

Clark, Willow.
  The true story of the Declaration of Independence / by Willow Clark. — 1st ed.
      p. cm. — (What really happened?)
  Includes index.
  ISBN 978-1-4488-9691-2 (library binding) — ISBN 978-1-4488-9840-4 (pbk.) —
  ISBN 978-1-4488-9841-1 (6-pack)
  1. United States. Declaration of Independence—Juvenile literature. 2. United States—History—Colonial period, ca. 1600–1775—Juvenile literature. 3. United States—History—Revolution, 1775–1783—Juvenile literature. 4. United States—Politics and government—1775–1783—Juvenile literature. I. Title.
  E221.C53 2013
  973.3'13—dc23
                                             2012029969

Manufactured in the United States of America

CPSIA Compliance Information: Batch #W13PK4: For Further Information contact Rosen Publishing, New York, New York at 1-800-237-9932

CONTENTS

DECLARING INDEPENDENCE

Every year on July 4, Americans celebrate Independence Day. It was on this day in 1776 that the American **colonies** adopted the Declaration of Independence. This **document** was the colonies' official announcement that they would no longer be ruled by Great Britain.

The Declaration of Independence is important because it stated why the people of the colonies believed they had the right to be free of British rule. It also argued that people had a right to choose their own government. The ideas in the Declaration of Independence are the same ideas on which the United States would be founded.

These kids are celebrating Independence Day. Though many people think that the Declaration of Independence was signed on July 4, it is actually the day it was adopted.

THE 13 COLONIES

The relationship between Great Britain and the 13 colonies became strained after the **French and Indian War** ended in 1763. This was a war with France over the control of North America. Britain's **Parliament** passed new **taxes** to help pay for the war.

These taxes were unpopular with the colonists. Colonists were also unhappy that they had no **representatives** in Parliament to speak up about laws and taxes that affected them. They thought of themselves as British subjects with the right to have representatives in Parliament.

The colonists **protested** the new laws and taxes passed by Parliament. These disagreements would lead to the **American Revolution**.

One of the things that the British taxed was tea. Colonists in Boston protested this by dressing up as Native Americans and dumping tea from ships into Boston Harbor.

WAR BREAKS OUT

In 1774, representatives from 12 of the 13 colonies met in Philadelphia, Pennsylvania. The group was known as the First Continental Congress. Its members discussed how the colonies should respond to the Coercive Acts. These were laws that punished the colonies for protesting Parliament's laws and taxes.

The tensions between Great Britain and the colonies turned to war on April 19, 1775. On that day, colonists successfully fought British troops at the Battles of Lexington and Concord, in Massachusetts. Though people sometimes think the Declaration of Independence started the war, more than a year would pass before it was written!

Fighting first broke out between colonists and British troops as the British marched through Lexington on their way to seize military supplies in Concord.

MEETING IN PHILADELPHIA

Representatives from each of the colonies met again starting in 1775 as the Second Continental Congress to discuss the war effort. They set up an army, called the Continental army, and put it under the command of George Washington.

Many people in the congress hoped to avoid a bigger war with Great Britain or to remain part of the British colonies. In July, Congress sent a letter to Britain's king, George III, asking for a peaceful solution. The king rejected this letter in August. As the fighting continued into the next spring, the congress met again to discuss whether a permanent break from Britain was necessary.

The Second Continental Congress met at the Pennsylvania Statehouse, in Philadelphia, Pennsylvania. Today it is known as Independence Hall.

DEBATING INDEPENDENCE

At the start of the American Revolution, most colonists did not want independence from Britain. As the war went on, Colonial support for independence grew. Colonists who were for independence were called Patriots, while those who were not were called Loyalists. Historians estimate that as many as 20 percent of the colonists remained Loyalists throughout the war.

Not every representative in the Second Continental Congress had permission from his colony's government to declare independence. However, by May 1776, the governments of eight colonies had voted for independence. The governments of Delaware, Maryland, New Jersey, New York, and Pennsylvania were holding back on declaring independence.

After the American Revolution ended, many Loyalists left the United States and moved to what is now Canada. This painting shows a group of Loyalists landing there.

WRITING THE DECLARATION

On June 7, 1776, Richard Henry Lee of Virginia presented a **resolution** to the Second Continental Congress. It said the colonies were "free and independent states."

Voting on the Lee Resolution was put off until July 2 because the congress was still waiting for support for independence from the five remaining colonies. In the meantime, the congress chose Thomas Jefferson, aided by John Adams, Benjamin Franklin, Robert Livingston, and Roger Sherman, to write a formal statement based on the Lee Resolution. This statement would list the reasons why the colonies were breaking away from Britain. It would become known as the Declaration of Independence.

This painting shows Franklin (left), Adams (middle), and Jefferson (right) working on the Declaration of Independence.

WHAT DOES IT SAY?

The Declaration of Independence says that the colonies need to declare independence. It also says that they have the natural right to do this.

It outlines the colonists' beliefs that "all men are created equal" and have the right to "life, liberty, and the pursuit of happiness." It says that governments are formed or revolted against to protect these rights. Then it lists the colonists' complaints, such as being taxed without Parliamentary representation. It finishes by saying that, because these complaints have been ignored, the colonies are ending their ties to Britain and declaring themselves "free and independent states."

Though the Declaration of Independence stated that the 13 colonies were declaring themselves free from Great Britain, it did not say they were forming a new nation.

WHAT HAPPENED WHEN?

The Declaration of Independence as we know it came together over a period of time. On July 28, 1776, Thomas Jefferson presented the draft he and the four other representatives wrote to the Second Continental Congress. The congress spent the next week discussing and making changes. They officially adopted the Declaration of Independence on July 4.

The Declaration of Independence was printed in the *Pennsylvania Evening Post* on July 6. The first public reading was in Philadelphia on July 8. It was only on August 2, 1776, that the Declaration of Independence was officially signed by the Continental Congress.

John Hancock was the first person to sign the Declaration of Independence. He was the president of the Continental Congress at the time it was signed.

INSPIRING DEMOCRACY

The Declaration of Independence marked the first time that people had made a written statement that they had the right to choose how they were governed. This idea is known as **democracy**. The **Constitution** is the foundation of the United States' government. It expands on the democratic ideas found in the Declaration of Independence.

The Declaration of Independence also had an impact on other countries that had revolutions to change their governments to democratic governments. One example is France. This country helped the colonies during the American Revolution. In 1789, the French Revolution started. It replaced France's king with a democratic government.

The American Revolution continued for several years after the Declaration of Independence was adopted. Fighting lasted until October 1781. The treaty that ended the war was signed in September 1783.

WHAT REALLY HAPPENED?

The Declaration of Independence is famous, but some facts about it are less so. Did you know that New York did not adopt the Declaration of Independence on July 4? It sat out the vote and adopted the declaration on July 15.

What we know about the writing of the Declaration of Independence is limited by what was left behind. Our knowledge is based on newspaper articles, letters, drafts, and other writing by the people involved. These give us a picture of events, but that picture is never complete. We could still discover facts that add to our knowledge of this historical event.

GLOSSARY

American Revolution (uh-MER-uh-ken reh-vuh-LOO-shun) Battles that soldiers from the colonies fought against Britain for freedom, from 1775 to 1783.

colonies (KAH-luh-neez) New places where people move that are still ruled by the leaders of the country from which they came.

Constitution (kon-stih-TOO-shun) The basic rules by which the United States is governed.

democracy (dih-MAH-kruh-see) A government that is run by the people who live under it.

document (DOK-yoo-ment) A written or printed statement that gives official information about something.

French and Indian War (FRENCH AND IN-dee-un WOR) The battles fought between 1754 and 1763 by England, France, and Native Americans for control of North America.

Parliament (PAR-leh-ment) The group in England that makes the country's laws.

protested (pruh-TEST-ed) Acted out in disagreement of something.

representatives (reh-prih-ZEN-tuh-tivz) People picked to speak for others.

resolution (reh-zuh-LOO-shun) A formal statement adopted by a group of people.

taxes (TAKS-ez) Money added to the price of things or paid to a government for community services.

INDEX

C
colonists, 6, 8, 12

F
France, 6, 20

G
government(s), 4, 12, 16, 20
Great Britain, 4, 6, 8, 10

I
idea(s), 4, 20

Independence Day, 4

L
laws, 6, 8

N
North America, 6

P
Parliament, 6
Philadelphia, Pennsylvania, 8, 18

R
relationship, 6
resolution, 14
right(s), 4, 6, 16, 20
rule, 4

S
subjects, 6

T
taxes, 6, 8
tensions, 8
troops, 8

WEBSITES

Due to the changing nature of Internet links, PowerKids Press has developed an online list of websites related to the subject of this book. This site is updated regularly. Please use this link to access the list:
www.powerkidslinks.com/wrh/inde/